FEAR IS NOT A SIN

FEAR IS NOT A SIN

It Is a Call to Action

Edward T. Welch

New Growth Press
newgrowthpress.com

New Growth Press, Greensboro, NC 27401
newgrowthpress.com
Copyright © 2025 Edward T. Welch

All rights reserved. No part of this publication may be reproduced, stored in a retrieval system, or transmitted in any form by any means, electronic, mechanical, photocopy, recording, or otherwise, without the prior permission of the publisher, except as provided by USA copyright law.

Unless otherwise indicated, Scripture quotations are taken from The ESV® Bible (The Holy Bible, English Standard Version®). ESV® Text Edition: 2016. Copyright © 2001 by Crossway, a publishing ministry of Good News Publishers. The ESV® text has been reproduced in cooperation with and by permission of Good News Publishers. Unauthorized reproduction of this publication is prohibited. All rights reserved.

Scripture quotations marked NIV are taken from The Holy Bible, New International Version®, NIV® Copyright © 1973, 1978, 1984, 2011 by Biblica, Inc.® Used by permission of Zondervan. All rights reserved worldwide. www.zondervan.com The "NIV" and "New International Version" are trademarks registered in the United States Patent and Trademark Office by Biblica, Inc.™

Scripture quotations marked CSB are taken from The Christian Standard Bible. Copyright © 2017 by Holman Bible Publishers. Used by permission. Christian Standard Bible ®, and CSB ® are federally registered trademarks of Holman Bible Publishers, all rights reserved.

Cover Design: Tim Green, Tiny Giant Co
Interior Typesetting/Ebook: Lisa Parnell, lparnellbookservices.com

ISBN: 978-1-64507-567-7 (paperback)
ISBN: 978-1-64507-568-4 (ebook)

Library of Congress Cataloging-in-Publication Data on file

Printed in the United States of America

29 28 27 26 25   1 2 3 4 5

To Mike Emlet
whose wisdom and love
are salt and light
to me and all who know him

CONTENTS

Chapter 1
A Command Is Not Always a Command 1

Chapter 2
A Desire Is Not Always a Sinful Desire 11

Chapter 3
God Meets Our Fears with Compassion
and Invites Us to Grow in Faith 23

Chapter 4
Growing Faith Includes Courage
and Confidence 37

Chapter 5
Sins to Watch for When Fearful and Anxious 55

CHAPTER ONE

A Command Is Not Always a Command

I was invited to talk about fear and anxiety on a radio program. After a few minutes, the host declared that after he received the Spirit he was never anxious again. I responded that after I received the Spirit, I never had a day without some kind of anxiety. For the remainder of the program, he insisted that I could not really be a Christian.

You are probably more like me than you are like the radio host. You know Jesus, and you know fears and anxiety. You also imagine that you will have those anxieties, either quietly in the background or roaring for your attention, for the rest of your life. This, of feel it in your body, but your body doesn't always get specific. You feel "stressed," and it is because of everything. The physical experience can be so intense you want to jump out of your own skin. Most of us are willing to try anything to escape that feeling.

The plan here is to enter into that fight. Fear and anxiety are not sinful. Left unattended, however, they can be dangerous. If you don't bring them to Jesus, you are left trusting in yourself, which *is* sin, and that will choke your soul (Mark 4:19). You want none of that. The plan will include crying out to the Lord, growing in our knowledge of him, and taking time to hear some of God's good and surprising words to you so you can take a wise stand when fears and anxieties get especially loud. To help you do that, each chapter in this short book will end with an opportunity to cry out to God and ask him for the help you need as you live in a fearful world.

This Command Is a Comfort

Yes, the words "Do not be afraid" are in the imperative or command form, along with "You shall not murder" or "You shall not steal." But a command is not always a command. Consider our common use of the phrase "Don't be afraid." It is *never* considered a command.

Take time to hear some of God's good and surprising words to you so you can take a wise stand when fears and anxieties get especially loud.

A Command Is Not Always a Command

We had a family living with us who had a five-year-old son. One day, I was playing with him in our backyard and I thought he might enjoy a walk through the woods that are right behind us. It would be an adventure. I put him on my shoulders and off we went. Within the first five steps, he began to cry. I responded, "Don't be afraid. I will make sure you are safe." It meant nothing to him, and he cried harder. But I didn't interpret it as rebellion. He was being a five-year-old who was in an unpredictable woods, in which there were all kinds of animals with teeth. When we say, "Don't be afraid" to children, it is the equivalent of "I am here; everything will be okay." If they cry, we don't rebuke them. We hold them.

Jesus has a similar intent. When he approaches a grieving widow in the village of Nain, "he had compassion on her and said to her, 'Do not weep'" (Luke 7:13). His words, though technically in the imperative form, are not a command, but an expression of care and compassion. He does not *require* something of her. Throughout his ministry when Jesus says, "Don't be afraid" or "Do not weep," it means that something good is about to happen. His compassion is aroused. He is going to help in a way that only he can.

When Jesus talks to his friends who were genuinely worried about the big things of life—food, clothing, shelter—his words are gentle. "Do not be afraid, little flock, for your Father has been pleased to give you the kingdom" (Luke 12:32 NIV). Compare this with Jesus's response to those who live with unconfessed sin. He warns "blind guides" and "hypocrites" (Matthew 23:13–29). He grieves over rebellion (Luke 13:34). When sin is clear and chronic, he does not typically speak of his vulnerable "little flock" and say, "I am with you."

The command form in Greek[1] can be used to present a request *or* make an appeal.[2] It includes a more moderate and softened version that is used in prayer. For example, the petitions in the Lord's Prayer are in the imperative form: "*Give us* this day our daily bread and *forgive us* our debts." But these petitions are not commands. Rather, they reveal our desires and intentions. When you hear the "commands" about fear and anxiety in Scripture, at least do this: Stop and listen. Jesus cares deeply about your fears, and he is going to say something important to you.

---

1. Greek is the original language of the New Testament.
2. E.g., Daniel B. Wallace, *Greek Grammar: Beyond the Basics* (Zondervan, 1996), 487.

REFLECT
&
JOURNAL

Read Psalm 23

The Lord is my shepherd; I shall not want.
  He makes me lie down in green pastures.
He leads me beside still waters.
  He restores my soul.
He leads me in paths of righteousness
  for his name's sake.
Even though I walk through the valley of the shadow of death,
  I will fear no evil,
for you are with me;
  your rod and your staff,
  they comfort me.
You prepare a table before me
  in the presence of my enemies;
you anoint my head with oil;
  my cup overflows.
Surely goodness and mercy shall follow me
  all the days of my life,
and I shall dwell in the house of the Lord
  forever.

REFLECT & JOURNAL

Using Psalm 23, write down five things about your good Shepherd that encourages you when you are afraid.

REFLECT & JOURNAL

Rewrite Psalm 23 into your prayer to God telling him about your worries and concerns and asking him to be your Shepherd.

CHAPTER TWO

A Desire Is Not Always a Sinful Desire

We might try to manage our anxiety by not thinking about it, which, of course, is impossible. But consider a different strategy. Let's take a hard look. Underneath fears and anxieties are personal desires that are at risk. We are anxious about a job interview because a poor interview jeopardizes our financial future. We are anxious about the results of a biopsy because cancer can be life-threatening. Fears identify what we want, what is important to us, and what we desire. If such desires are always wrong, fear is sinful. But such desires are not always wrong.

The Old Testament speaks of natural, human desires:

> What is desired in a man is steadfast love. (Proverbs 19:22)
>
> I am my beloved's, and his desire is for me. (Song of Solomon 7:10)
>
> You satisfy the desire of the afflicted. (Isaiah 58:10)

The Bible certainly has its warnings about misplaced and unleashed desires, but Scripture attests that to be human is to have desire. Fears identify those things that are important to you.

Among our natural desires are life and health, food and shelter, love, enough money to care for ourselves and our families, peace in relationships, freedom from injustice and oppression, and a good reputation. The New Testament assumes natural desires (Luke 22:15) yet emphasizes our tendency to always want more. This emphasis gives us opportunity to consider if our fears are built on *excessive* desires. What makes them excessive is when we love them more than we love Jesus. When we notice that is true, we turn and ask for forgiveness. But not all desires are excessive. And the presence of natural desires means that, in an uncertain world, we have good reasons to be afraid.

The experience of grief is a helpful analogy. Grief is fear's mirror twin. Fear is a desire that is threatened; grief is a desire taken away. Fear is when a loved one's diagnosis is uncertain; grief is when a loved one dies. A life without grief is a life without love. The apostle Paul was distressed over a dear friend's illness. When he recovered, Paul wrote that Epaphroditus's death would have caused him "sorrow upon sorrow" (Philippians 2:27), and no one would have begrudged him such grief. Grief is met with compassion rather than suspicion of reckless desires. Fear, too, is met with compassion. The Lord expects us to be afraid.

The Lord Expects Us to Be Afraid

Some people seem to be fearless. There are countless stories of men and women who were heroic, which means they placed their life in jeopardy in order to serve other people. When you hear the details of those stories, the heroes sound quite mortal. They were afraid, but love and a mission would not let fear stop them from what they desired even more, just as you would act in heroic ways if someone you love needed help.

Is it possible to live without fear and anxiety? Perhaps, but it would be a severe pathology that also left you without love. Such a life would mean that your soul is dead. It would not signal your great faith. Quite the opposite. It would reveal that life had lost all meaning, you had abandoned all hope, God was irrelevant, and you simply didn't care anymore.

Scripture assumes that we live with fear and anxiety. We are weak people who can control very little. Our reputation, finances, loved ones, and even our lives are at risk every day. The Psalms are filled with human fears and anxieties—and these are words that the Lord asks us to speak to him. He actually wants to hear about our fears.

> My heart is in anguish within me; the terrors of death have fallen upon me. Fear and trembling come upon me, and horror overwhelms me. And I say, "Oh, that I had wings like a dove! I would fly away and be at rest." (Psalm 55:4–6)

The Psalms are filled with human fears and anxieties—and these are words that the Lord asks us to speak to him. He actually wants to hear about our fears.

> How long, O LORD? Will you forget me forever? How long will you hide your face from me? How long must I take counsel in my soul and have sorrow in my heart all the day? How long shall my enemy be exalted over me? (Psalm 13:1–2)

> The cords of death encompassed me; the torrents of destruction assailed me; the cords of Sheol entangled me; the snares of death confronted me. In my distress I called upon the LORD. (Psalm 18:4–6)

> My heart is like wax; it is melted within my breast. (Psalm 22:14)

These are not confessions of sin. They are confessions that we truly do need the Lord, and such dependence pleases him.

The apostle Paul also acknowledges his fears. "For even when we came into Macedonia, our bodies had no rest, but we were afflicted at every turn—fighting without and *fear within*" (2 Corinthians 7:5, emphasis added). God's comfort came in the person of Titus and in his report that the churches were following the words that Paul had written to them.

Fear and anxiety express our weakness amid the threats of daily life. We are merely human—finite, limited, and weak. We are not the Creator. Weak people are also sinners, but *weakness is not sin.* Weakness means that we need help from God and other people. The good news is that God's help is available to all who ask. You can start by asking right now for the help you need.

*The good news
is that God's help
is available
to all who ask.*

REFLECT & JOURNAL

Read the following verses.

In my distress I called upon the LORD; to my God I cried for help. From his temple he heard my voice, and my cry to him reached his ears. (Psalm 18:6)

But you, O LORD, do not be far off! O you my help, come quickly to my aid! (Psalm 22:19)

Our soul waits for the LORD; he is our help and our shield. (Psalm 33:20)

When the righteous cry for help, the LORD hears and delivers them out of all their troubles. (Psalm 34:17)

My help comes from the LORD, who made heaven and earth. (Psalm 121:2)

REFLECT & JOURNAL

Write one or two things from each verse that you have learned about God (they can be the same things).

REFLECT & JOURNAL

Write down one specific fear that troubles you today. Speak those troubles to God and ask for his strength.

CHAPTER THREE

God Meets Our Fears with Compassion and Invites Us to Grow in Faith

Throughout the Old Testament, God made covenants with his people. A covenant from God is a formal promise to care for and never leave his people. They were made or reaffirmed when God's people were in uncertain times and had reason to be afraid. In response, the Lord gave assurances of his care in the most vivid and meaningful way possible. Think of a human pact where you double and triple swear, or you even take out a knife and cut your palm, sealing the agreement in blood. In other words, when you are anxious, God hears you and is eager that *you* hear his commitment and promises.

Notice the Lord's renewal of his covenant with Abraham with his grandson Jacob. Jacob was a liar who had cheated his brother Esau out of his inheritance. His victimized brother had reason to be angry with him. When Jacob's parents realized that his life was at risk because of Esau's anger, they sent him to live with his great-uncle Laban, where he would hopefully find a wife and receive protection. On the way, the Lord met him in a dream and said this to him:

> "Behold, I am with you and will keep you wherever you go, and will bring you back to this land [which I will give to you and your offspring]. For I will not leave you until I have done what I have promised you." (Genesis 28:15)

To a man who deserved rebuke, the Lord focused on Jacob's fear and led with comfort: "I am with you. . . . I will not leave you." Get accustomed to those words. They are the key words the Lord spoke to Jacob and speaks to you. The Lord committed to be faithful and present, even when Jacob was less so.

In the New Testament, Jesus's words continue this tradition of assurance and comfort. In the Gospels of both Luke and Matthew, Jesus says, "Do not be anxious about your life" (Matthew 6:25; Luke 12:22). Remember how in Luke's account, Jesus concludes with this: "Fear not, little flock, for it is your Father's good pleasure to give you the kingdom" (12:32). Jesus sees us as vulnerable sheep needing his care. His words are gentle and affectionate. Do you have doubts? He wants you to remember that he only speaks the truth. He will do what he says. His double swear is his death and resurrection on your behalf. Our fears, in truth, arouse his compassion—not his rebuke. "He has pity on the weak and the needy. . . . For he knows our frame; he remembers that we are dust" (Psalm 72:13; 103:14).

From "Little Faith" to Fuller Faith

These passages are clear. When you hear them, you are able to speak to Jesus with more confidence rather than forget about him or shy away from him in shame. This is exactly what you need. Speak to him. This is the right path.

Then you hear Jesus give you a nudge. "O you of little faith" (Luke 12:28; Matthew 6:30). That appears only one time in Luke. But Matthew uses it five times

Jesus sees us as vulnerable sheep needing his care. His words are gentle and affectionate. . . . He wants you to remember that he only speaks the truth.

in his Gospel, including when the disciples are afraid in a boat that seems to be sinking (8:26), when Peter walked on a tumultuous sea and began to sink (14:31), and when the disciples could not heal a demon-possessed man (17:20). In the context of the story of the demon-possessed man, Jesus also says that faith the size of a mustard seed can move mountains. A mustard seed is tiny, so your "little-faith" must, indeed, be small.

The word *faith* can have different meanings. *The faith* can be identical to *the gospel*, the story of Jesus who came to rescue us through his death and resurrection. Faith is also the common way that the Bible identifies our trust in Jesus. It is an action or our response to him. It never stands alone, as in "just have faith." It is always, "put your trust *in* Jesus." For the word *faith*, you could substitute *confidence*, *hope*, *trust*, or *rest* in Jesus. A third use of the word *faith* is that faith is a quantity or amount. People are described as having more faith or less faith. Jesus uses the phrase "little faith" as a description. It also could be heard as an alternate name, "little-faith."

To be sure, little-faiths are followers of Jesus. They listen to his teaching and they even follow him into small boats when the forecast is for storms. They are his people and even their limited faith can move mountains. Notice the disciples' little, but very real, faith while they are in the storm (Matthew 8:23–27). Rather than simply panic, they wake Jesus and cry out for help, "Save us, Lord; we are perishing." Three simple words in Greek: "Lord, save-us, we-perish." A childlike appeal. This is faith.

I have called each of my grandchildren "little-one" during some phase of their lives. It is an expression of my fondness and even enjoyment of their need for help that I can provide. Jesus does something similar when he says, "Fear not, little flock." The task of little-faiths is to rest in Jesus and *grow*. We pray, "Increase our faith!" (Luke 17:5). We want our fears to be joined to courage and confidence that he is with us, and we always want more of that courage and confidence.

The apostle Peter uses a similar idea but with love rather than faith. "Having purified your souls by your obedience to the truth for a sincere brotherly love, love one another earnestly from a pure heart" (1 Peter 1:22). That is, you have love for your brothers—you are on the right path—now grow in even more love. When sin is the primary problem, you turn from it. You change course because you are on the wrong path. Here, you are encouraged to stay the current course that keeps you moving with and toward Jesus.

Along the way, you meet those with greater faith. They have all been in dire straits and have reasons for fear, yet they are heroes we hope to emulate. Watch for centurions (Matthew 8:10), friends of a paralytic (Matthew 9:2), a woman who touched Jesus's garment (Matthew 9:22), a Canaanite woman (Matthew 15:28), and many others who Jesus healed. The Spirit of God has been known to use other people to inspire you.

The writer of Hebrews mentions many who were "commended through their faith" (Hebrews 11:39). There are some surprising names on the list, including Gideon and Samson. These two men would seem to barely make the little-faith list. Gideon was a coward and idolater; Samson was foolish. Yet, when you look closely at their stories, you discover a mustard seed of faith. Gideon "worshiped" after receiving a third sign from the Lord that he would deliver the Midianites into Israel's hand, and he went into battle with courage (Judges 7:15). Samson "called to the Lord" (Judges 16:28) after he was captured by the Philistines. These small acts of faith were accompanied by God's large acts of deliverance.

God has determined to use little-faith to accomplish his mission. In this, he shows the world that he delivers through his strength. We in turn witness that he is indeed with us, and he uses us in our weakness. Then, notice that your fears and worries are not quite as stuck. Hope grows. Faith grows. A vision takes shape—fuzzy, but a vision all the same—and a vision likes to take action. Perhaps little-faith can be growing-faith and even big-faith. And it can, as "my soul finds rest in God alone" (Psalm 62:1 NIV 1984).

**REFLECT
&
JOURNAL**

Read these Matthew stories about little faith:

And when he got into the boat, his disciples followed him. And behold, there arose a great storm on the sea, so that the boat was being swamped by the waves; but he was asleep. And they went and woke him, saying, "Save us, Lord; we are perishing." And he said to them, "Why are you afraid, O you of little faith?" Then he rose and rebuked the winds and the sea, and there was a great calm. (Matthew 8:23–26)

And in the fourth watch of the night he came to them, walking on the sea. But when the disciples saw him walking on the sea, they were terrified, and said, "It is a ghost!" and they cried out in fear. But immediately Jesus spoke to them, saying, "Take heart; it is I. Do not be afraid." And Peter answered him, "Lord, if it is you, command me to come to you on the water." He said, "Come." So Peter got out of the boat and walked on the water and came to Jesus. But when he saw the wind, he was afraid, and beginning to sink he cried out, "Lord, save me." Jesus immediately reached out his hand and took hold of him, saying to him, "O you of little faith, why did you doubt?" And when they got into the boat, the wind ceased. And those in the boat worshiped him, saying, "Truly you are the Son of God." (Matthew 14:25–33)

And when they came to the crowd, a man came up to him and, kneeling before him, said, "Lord, have mercy on my son, for he has seizures and he suffers terribly. For often he falls into the fire, and often into the water. And I brought him to your disciples, and they could not heal him." And Jesus answered, "O faithless and twisted generation, how long am I to be with you? How long am I to bear with you? Bring him here to me." And Jesus rebuked the demon, and it came out of him, and the boy was healed instantly. Then the disciples came to Jesus privately and said, "Why could we not cast it out?" He said to them, "Because of your little faith. For truly, I say to you, if you have faith like a grain of mustard seed, you will say to this mountain, 'Move from here to there,' and it will move, and nothing will be impossible for you." (Matthew 17:14–20)

REFLECT & JOURNAL

What do you learn about people with little faith? How does Jesus interact with "little-faiths"?

REFLECT & JOURNAL

What do you learn from these stories about how to talk to God when you are afraid?

REFLECT & JOURNAL

Now write a "little-faith" prayer to Jesus expressing your need. Can you also ask him to grow your faith?

CHAPTER FOUR

Growing Faith Includes Courage and Confidence

Fear is always a time to grow in faith. That growth is usually as simple as saying, "Jesus help!" This is what you want to master during your fears and anxieties. "Be gracious to me, O God, for man tramples on me" (Psalm 56:1). If you make this a habit, your faith will strengthen and mature and you will come to have greater courage and confidence. Together they can feel like rest.

Courage

Growth in courage will not abolish fear, but it might help you be less paralyzed in the midst of it.

Remember, courage is not the absence of fear, but it is how we persevere in what we know is right and good despite being afraid.

Fear takes many forms. Consider a time when you avoided a conversation because it was relationally risky. Let's say that your spouse, or someone with whom you have a close relationship, has wronged you and you believe it would be best to speak about it. But you are anxious. You risk the possibility of anger and a larger rift in the relationship. Courage means that you speak even though you fear the outcome.

Or consider something more severe. So much of our fear is connected to death. Here again you can be courageous, even as you have fears. Courage can be outweighed by love and duty. One of my vivid memories from childhood was when my older sister fell into a pond, and my father, lame from polio and a poor swimmer, immediately cast off his crutches and ran into the water to rescue her. That image of love conquering fear has never left me.

This kind of courage *sounds* good. You can almost hear other people saying to you, "Go ahead; I did it. You can do it. Keep going. Face those fears." But you can't. Proceed carefully in this one because you might be heading off into some significant dangers. You can detect those dangers when you are discouraged and feeling hopeless, when you no longer hear God's words of comfort, or when you see little point in talking with him. *This* is real danger. When you see it, there is a simple way out. That way is not self-talk, "I can do this. I can do this. C'mon just do it." Notice that you don't really need Jesus to do that. Instead, the path to courageous faith insists that you talk to Jesus more than you talk to yourself.

Courageous faith cries out, "Lord, save me." That is courage. So we call out to the Lord when we are in peril. Then, we call out again. When we stop and consider our God—both his love and faithfulness fully made known to us in Jesus Christ—it nurtures us and nudges us forward in faith. We hear Jesus say, "Take heart; it is I" (Matthew 14:27), and we add to our cries, "Yes, Lord, I believe." But still, "help."

Though we can conjure up troubles in the future that never come to pass, there are real troubles that surround us. The psalmists often are delivered from their foes, but foes *can* overtake us. We fear that a loved one might die, and the loved one dies. We fear being alone, and we are actually quite alone. Our troubles are a consequence of a lingering curse on creation and they arouse the compassion of the Lord. But these troubles are also "a testing of your faith" that exposes little faith and grows our faith to be "perfect and complete" (James 1:3–4). They are occasions to grow in courage, in which we are more certain that God is with us, that death will not have the final word, and that Jesus has overcome the world (John 16:33). Then, having spoken to Jesus about our predicament, we ask him to help us to take one little step. He has given each of us a mission that includes love and work, and he gives us power to do *something*. Fears and anxiety naturally leave us paralyzed or engaged in activities that avoid what is most important. Little-faiths ask the Lord for power for one little next step of faith and love. If that little step is unclear, we ask a good friend to help us.

Confidence

Another way Scripture speaks of growing faith is as confidence in Jesus (Ephesians 3:12; Hebrews 10:35). I stepped into an old boat recently that was headed for rocky waters. Among our small party, I was the only one who seemed unafraid or at least unaffected by the combination of a rickety boat and bigger seas. My secret was that I knew and trusted our skipper. He had navigated that same course countless times, and he was unconcerned. If he was not afraid, I was not afraid. In a similar way, the better we know Jesus, the more our words to him will combine a description of

When we stop and consider our God—both his love and faithfulness fully made known to us in Jesus Christ—it nurtures us and nudges us forward in faith.

our fears and a recounting of how we know that he is trustworthy.

Keep your conversation with him going, like the Psalms themselves. They can begin with a cry for help, and then say a bit more.

> When I am afraid, I put my trust in you. In God, whose word I praise, in God I trust; I shall not be afraid. What can flesh do to me? (Psalm 56:3–4)

> Though an army encamp against me, my heart shall not fear; though war arise against me, yet I will be confident.... For he will hide me in his shelter in the day of trouble; he will conceal me under the cover of his tent; he will lift me high upon a rock. (Psalm 27:3, 5)

Psalms begin with fear, move toward the faithfulness of the Lord, and end with confidence and hope. If you stop after your cry for help, that is faith. Perhaps next time you can join the psalmists who remind you that he has helped and will help, and your confidence will grow, and you say more.

This confidence in Jesus is also the message of 1 John. John, the author, is certainly familiar with fears that come from dangerous circumstances. But he aims for something more. The critical questions are these. Can you be sure that you are not alone in the midst of one danger after another? Is Jesus with you and does he care? Simply put, does he really care *for you*? That is a recurring question in Scripture. Confidence grows when you hear that question from Jesus himself, and you keep talking until you say to him, "Yes, I believe you care."

Your answer is grounded in this: Jesus has taken your sins on himself and taken them away. Your sins were the only thing that could keep you from him, and sin no longer has that power. Jesus is now your advocate before the Father. When you confess sin, you can be certain he forgives you. When you put your faith in him, you have evidence that you are a child of God. He abides in you and you in him, and he will never abandon his children. Never. So you can have confident hope.

> And now, little children, abide in him, so that when he appears we may have confidence and not shrink from him in shame at his coming. (1 John 2:28)

> Beloved, if our heart does not condemn us, we have confidence before God. (1 John 3:21)

Guilt can tell you that Jesus has had enough of you. When guilt persists, and fears attach to that guilt, you have misunderstood God's fatherly love and the cleansing work of Jesus. God is love, yet your fears anticipate punishment (1 John 4:18). The message to you, instead, is of joy, belonging, and confidence in the day of judgment. You are God's child *now* (1 John 3:2). As beloved children, John urges you walk with that confidence.

The apostle Paul identifies this confidence as a clear conscience (Acts 24:16; 1 Timothy 3:9). A clear conscience does not mean sinless, but it does mean that you are open with the Lord about your sins, confess them, and rest in his forgiveness. As you remember what Jesus has done, you are persuaded that he hears and forgives you when you call out to him (1 John 5:14).

Jonah might help you here. He was truly going against God's direct command, ending up at sea, which would surely take his life. But that was interrupted by being swallowed by a fish, which only seemed like a gross postponement of the inevitable. However, this deliverance from the sea reminded Jonah that God had not abandoned him. Instead, God followed Jonah on his escape boat, into the sea, and into the fish. In other words, *Jonah's sins would not separate him from the God who cares.* The Lord had forgiven him. So Jonah could speak a psalm of praise to the Lord because his presence was enough (Jonah 2:1–9).

Fear is *always* a time to grow in faith. As you seek his help, God uses your trials to mature you from a little-faith to a big-faith. As you take little steps, there are, indeed, real dangers. They are reasons to cry out to the Lord and speak about these dangers, and you might fear those dangers in your very bones. They are also an occasion for something that begins to feel like an adventure. God is with you and is doing something good. You begin to look for the form his deliverance takes. Read these verses again and notice they speak of how God will deliver in trouble.

> When I am afraid, I put my trust in you. In God, whose word I praise, in God I trust; I shall not be afraid. What can flesh do to me? (Psalm 56:1–4)

> Though an army encamp against me, my heart shall not fear; though war arise against me, yet I will be confident.... For he will hide me in his shelter in the day of trouble; he will conceal me under the cover of his tent; he will lift me high upon a rock. (Psalm 27:3, 5)

How have you seen God deliver you in the midst of fear and trouble? Growing in courage and confidence is always a work of the Spirit in our lives—and something you can ask for and then thank God for when you notice more courage and confidence today than you had yesterday.

Rest

Fears and anxieties often begin with a sense that you are alone and there is no one who loves you enough and is strong enough to help. Then you begin to talk to the Lord. You might simply describe to him the terror that you feel. You put words to your experience of being on the verge of panic. Those words feel like desperation; they are more accurately identified as faith. Gradually your conversations include your response to his question, *Do you believe I care for you?* In response, be sure to acknowledge Jesus—God's proof—and keep learning about him until you can say yes. All this means you are well on your way to being a big-faith.

Big-faiths always want more. More confidence in the presence and love of Jesus Christ, more courage as your mission unfolds in little steps. And there is more. One way you can honor the name of Jesus is to learn that you are on a journey in which he invites you to rest in him. The child honors the father when the child asks for help. Even more, the child honors the father when the child is sure the father is strong enough to do anything. The little one rests in an otherwise threatening place because the child knows the father is very near. "In peace I will both lie down and sleep; for you alone, O LORD, make me dwell in safety" (Psalm 4:8). You sleep; he stays awake.

Slow down for just a moment. How do you respond to what you have read so far? It should sound good—that is the easy part. It is also a call to action—that is the hard part. For that hard part, Peter reminds you of a powerful yet neglected skill: "humble yourselves" (1 Peter 5:6). Humility asks, Are you listening to the Lord? Really listening, so his words have more weight than your fears and worries. Your hope comes when you live under the voice of God. If you want that, tell Jesus. Ask for it, now.

One way you can honor the name of Jesus is to learn that you are on a journey in which he invites you to rest in him.

REFLECT
&
JOURNAL

Many psalms begin with fear, then move on to a cry for help, and finally celebrate God's faithfulness.

Read Psalm 28 below and circle those three elements (fear, a cry for help, and celebrating God's faithfulness) in the psalm:

Lord, I call to you;
my rock, do not be deaf to me.
If you remain silent to me,
I will be like those going down to the Pit.
Listen to the sound of my pleading
when I cry to you for help,
when I lift up my hands
toward your holy sanctuary.

Do not drag me away with the wicked,
with the evildoers,
who speak in friendly ways with their neighbors
while malice is in their hearts.
Repay them according to what they have done—
according to the evil of their deeds.

REFLECT & JOURNAL

Repay them according to the work of their hands;
give them back what they deserve.
Because they do not consider
what the Lord has done
or the work of his hands,
he will tear them down and not rebuild them.

Blessed be the Lord,
for he has heard the sound of my pleading.
The Lord is my strength and my shield;
my heart trusts in him, and I am helped.
Therefore my heart celebrates,
and I give thanks to him with my song.

The Lord is the strength of his people;
he is a stronghold of salvation for his anointed.
Save your people, bless your possession,
shepherd them, and carry them forever. (CSB)

REFLECT & JOURNAL

Now rewrite this psalm as your own prayer. Where David talks about his enemies, insert all that is troubling you and making you afraid.

REFLECT & JOURNAL

REFLECT & JOURNAL

CHAPTER FIVE

Sins to Watch for When Fearful and Anxious

This part should be relatively easy. If you have faced your fears and anxieties with Jesus, it is easy to face your sins. It is a no-lose deal. There is no, "How many times do I have to tell you?" Your awareness of sin and confession are met with unwavering love and forgiveness, and you provoke his delight because he both loves to forgive and he enjoys the closeness that confession always brings to a relationship. "Whoever comes to me I will never cast out" (John 6:37).

We need no occasion to confess sins. Jesus instructs us to speak our confession to him each day (Matthew 6:12). Pride and selfishness are always active in our hearts, even when no one else sees them. Our love for others is exceeded by our love for ourselves, and our love for God always falls short of being whole-hearted. Other times we can hear his good words to us but be unmoved by them or not believe them. There are always worthy matters of our hearts to confess, and such confession can always enhance our confidence and courage while it also has the seeds of joy embedded in it.

Fears and anxieties heighten our interest in confession. Consider how confession in the midst of fear can strengthen and help us. All suffering leaves us vulnerable to question God's care. When we confess sins we remember that he loves us even as our own love is cold, and he has fully forgiven us in Christ. Even in suffering, we have a rich hope that he makes us fruitful now and he will make all things new.

Fears and anxieties can choke spiritual life. Confession keeps us vigilant to Satan's lies about ourselves and God. Fear and anxieties are not sinful, but, like everything in life, your sin can get tangled up in it.

So, armed with a growing confidence that you are a forgiven sinner and nothing can separate you from Christ, you proceed with care.

Sin in Our Response to Fear

Fear and what we do with our fear are two different things. Fear is natural; our responses to fear can be more complicated, but they can be examined with one simple question: *Did I turn toward the Lord or not?* When you turn away, it can look like disobedience, complaining, or silence.

Disobedience

God commanded King Saul to destroy Amalek and everything associated with the city. But Saul "feared the people and obeyed their voice" (1 Samuel 15:24), and chose to spare the Amalekite king and the best of their animals. As a result, God took the kingship away from Saul and gave it to David. The Lord would likely sympathize with Saul if he had become unpopular for obeying him, and the Lord certainly would have invited Saul to speak with him about the predicament, but Saul violated God's direct and unequivocal command.

You rarely will be in a situation where your fears keep you from obeying a direct command from the Lord. But, since people familiar with fear and anxiety often have sensitive consciences, you might think you are guilty of *something*. Opt for a simple way through this. Disobedient people don't talk to the Lord. They

There are always worthy matters of our hearts to confess, and such confession can always enhance our confidence and courage while it also has the seeds of joy embedded in it.

Sins to Watch for When Fearful and Anxious

just do what they are going to do. So talk with him. Tell him what you don't understand. Look for psalms that guide you to good places. *Good* is critical to know. God's words to you are very good. They can be hard, but always good. Be sure to settle in that place where you have heard his words as they were intended to be hear, as good for you soul.

Complaining

After Israel left Egypt for the land God promised, they heard ominous reports about the new land's inhabitants: They were strong and lived in heavily fortified cities. The people, in response, were afraid. Their fear was not the problem. It was how they responded to their fear that was the problem. They cried and wished they had never left Egypt, which was another way of saying Pharaoh was a better guardian than the Lord (Numbers 14). They wanted to stone their leaders, and they didn't cry out to the Lord.

This response was sinful. Complaining doesn't sound like it is against God, but that is the point. It doesn't speak to him or acknowledge him.

> And the LORD said to Moses, "How long will this people despise me? And how long will they not believe in me, in spite

> of all the signs that I have done among them? I will strike them with the pestilence and disinherit them, and I will make of you a nation greater and mightier than they." (Numbers 14:11–12)

Once again, talk to God.

Silence

We might occasionally act in disobedience when we are afraid, but more often, if we have a sinful response, it will be *silence* before God. When we are afraid, it is not unusual to redouble our efforts, consider our options, and find new strategies. These are not wrong, but if our human effort is not accompanied by prayer, we are sinning in our silence. We act independently, as though we tried trusting God and it didn't work, so we rely on ourselves.

When the nation of Israel split into two, the northern kingdom was the first to be seriously threatened. In response, they cried out in fear—but *not* to the Lord. Instead, they trusted in foreign alliances rather than his protection, and they turned to idols and self-harm rituals to ensure their food supply.

King Ahaz followed this tradition of self-reliance when the southern kingdom was threatened. After the Lord gave assurances that the tribes who opposed Ahaz would not stand, the Lord asked for a response from Ahaz.

> The LORD spoke to Ahaz, "Ask a sign of the LORD your God; let it be deep as Sheol or high as heaven." But Ahaz said, "I will not ask, and I will not put the LORD to the test." (Isaiah 7:10–12)

Why wouldn't Ahaz ask for a sign? Because he trusted in his foreign alliances to protect him.

This does not mean that you never look for help from other people or medicine. King Asa is your teacher. "In his disease he did not seek the LORD, but sought help from physicians" (2 Chronicles 16:12). The problem was not that he sought help from physicians. It is that he sought help *only* from physicians.

Sin and What We Love Most

Fear is not sin because there are things and people you *should* desire or even love, and when they are threatened your life is upended. These loves, however, are part of a very delicate imbalance. You were made to love Jesus above all else, more than mother or father (Matthew 10:37), more than money (Matthew 6:24).

Whoever or whatever you love most will be your master. Fears and anxieties, as a result, are the ideal opportunity to ask some questions. Have your desires become too big? Desires are normal. Outsized desires are idols. Do you love health, money and reputation *above all else*? When fears and anxieties are especially loud, persistent, and frequent, look for overgrown desires that can be tangled up with them. The way through this morass is to speak about it to the Lord, confess it where you see it, and set out to know Jesus more accurately. When you know him well, you will love him more.

This brings us to a second question. The first is, "Do you believe I care for you?" The second is the question Jesus asked Peter. "Do you love me?" (John 21:16). Who would have thought that Jesus would ask you that very question as a way to quiet your anxieties? It gets to the very heart of your response to the love of Jesus. "You shall love the Lord your God with all your heart and with all your soul and with all your might" (Deuteronomy 6:5). Talk to him, believe what he says, and love him.

Fear in the Age of the Spirit

Jesus remains very aware of your vulnerabilities. Fears are to be expected, and they are consistently met by the God who hears and cares. We are his little flock and he does not minimize your worries. He is your high priest who sympathizes with your weaknesses and frailties (Hebrews 4:15). And when you are afraid, those fears become an occasion for the Lord to repeat his greatest promise to you: "I am with you." Your growth is measured *not* by the intensity of your fears and anxieties, but in how you turn to Jesus.

Indeed, he is always with you. Yet there is more. Because you live in the age of the Spirit, you are more active in response to your fears. You want to grow. You are a little-faith who hopes to honor the Lord with growing confidence, courage, and rest. During that growth, you expect to speak more openly to him, cry out for help with less delay, and learn from people of faith who came before you. You grow in confidence that Jesus loves you, that he is with you in the storms, and that he is very, very strong. You, in turn, speak to him, again and again. And listen. And love.

*When you are afraid,
those fears become
an occasion for the Lord
to repeat his greatest
promise to you:
"I am with you."*

REFLECT
&
JOURNAL

Psalm 130 reflects on God's forgivenesss and also brings all fears to the Lord and promises to wait for his deliverance. It's a psalm of ascents— God's people sang it every year on their way to the temple to worship. Read it through once or twice.

Out of the depths I cry to you, O Lord!
    O Lord, hear my voice!
Let your ears be attentive
    to the voice of my pleas for mercy!

If you, O Lord, should mark iniquities,
    O Lord, who could stand?
But with you there is forgiveness,
    that you may be feared.

I wait for the Lord, my soul waits,
    and in his word I hope;
my soul waits for the Lord
    more than watchmen for the morning,
    more than watchmen for the morning.

REFLECT & JOURNAL

O Israel, hope in the LORD!
    For with the LORD there is steadfast love,
    and with him is plentiful redemption.
And he will redeem Israel
    from all his iniquities.

Now rewrite it as your own pilgrim cry to God.

REFLECT & JOURNAL

REFLECT & JOURNAL

REFLECT & JOURNAL

ccef

CCEF is committed to restoring Christ to counseling and counseling to the church. They seek to accomplish this mission through resources, courses, events, and counseling.

To learn more or explore CCEF's resources, visit **ccef.org**.

MORE FROM EDWARD T. WELCH

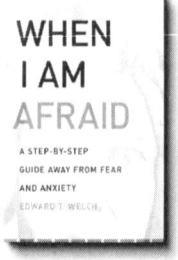

NEW GROWTH PRESS

newgrowthpress.com